SODA SCIENCE

Other Boston Children's Museum Activity Books
by Bernie Zubrowski

Balloons
Building and Experimenting with Inflatable Toys

Ball-Point Pens

Blinkers and Buzzers
Building and Experimenting with Electricity and Magnetism

Bubbles

Clocks
Building and Experimenting with Model Timepieces

Making Waves
Finding Out About Rhythmic Motion

Messing Around with Drinking Straw Construction

Messing Around with Water Pumps and Siphons

Milk Carton Blocks

Mirrors
Finding Out About the Properties of Light

Mobiles
Building and Experimenting with Balancing Toys

Raceways
Having Fun with Balls and Tracks

Shadow Play
Making Pictures with Light and Lenses

Tops
Building and Experimenting with Spinning Toys

Wheels at Work
Building and Experimenting with Models of Machines

SODA SCIENCE
DESIGNING AND TESTING SOFT DRINKS

BERNIE ZUBROWSKI

ILLUSTRATED BY **ROY DOTY**

A BOSTON CHILDREN'S MUSEUM ACTIVITY BOOK

A BEECH TREE PAPERBACK BOOK • NEW YORK

Printed in the United States of America.

The Library of Congress has cataloged the Morrow Junior Books edition of *Soda Science: Designing and Testing Soft Drinks* as follows:
Zubrowski, Bernie.
Soda science: designing and testing soft drinks/Bernie Zubrowski; illustrated by Roy Doty.
p. cm.—(A Boston Children's Museum activity book)
Summary: Explores how soft drinks are made, with experiments and activities that demonstrate the scientific principles involved.
ISBN 0-688-13917-5
1. Soft drinks—Juvenile literature. [1. Soft drinks—Experiments. 2. Experiments.] I. Doty, Roy.
II. Title. III. Series. TP630.Z83 1997 641.8'75—dc20 96-23735 CIP AC

1 3 5 7 9 10 8 6 4 2
First Beech Tree Edition, 1997
ISBN 0-688-13983-3

ACKNOWLEDGMENTS

Thanks to Susan Erickson, who checked the accuracy of the scientific content, and extraspecial thanks to Marjorie Waters, who helped me put the final manuscript into clear and coherent form. Also to the students and teachers at the McCarthy Towne School in Acton, Massachusetts, and to students at the Farragut School in Boston who helped me try out the projects in this book.

CONTENTS

SODA SCIENCE

INTRODUCTION

Sodas are very popular drinks all over the world. Millions of cans and bottles of soda are sold yearly. Each country has its own special flavors, but there are a few flavors, such as lemon and cola, that are universally popular. The next time you visit your local supermarket and walk down the aisle that has sodas, see how many different flavors are available.

Soda is mostly water, with flavoring, sugar, and gas added. Almost all of these ingredients are probably in your kitchen already. It can be great fun

mixing them together to see what combinations give the taste that you like the best. You can design a soda that is just for you. You can also test your recipe to see if other people like it, too.

In the process of making up recipes and carrying out experiments, you will begin to understand the chemical makeup of sodas as well as some of the chemical techniques used in making them.

SAFETY NOTE: Some of the experiments and activities will involve working with a stove and hot liquids. These activities should be done with an adult, so that he or she can help you follow the proper procedures.

THE INGREDIENTS

In most sodas, the ingredients are listed on the label. If you read those labels, you will find that some sodas are made with all-natural ingredients. These have flavoring, color, and sweetener that come from different kinds of fruit. Other sodas are a mixture of natural and artificial ingredients. For example, in these sodas the coloring is often a manufactured chemical rather than a natural substance. The flavors are also chemicals. So, before you start making up your own soda recipe, you should spend some time getting acquainted with the methods that are used to obtain the ingredients found in sodas.

In this chapter, you'll be doing a fun and interesting series of investigations to see how colors and flavors are *extracted*, or separated out of substances, from natural materials; how flavors can be *concentrated*, or made stronger; and how gas can be added to the final mixture to make the soda bubbly. In doing the investigations, you will learn about some of the physical and chemical properties of these materials.

EXTRACTING NATURAL COLOR

You probably already know that tea bags release the flavor and color of their contents into hot water and that pouring hot water into paper filters containing ground coffee makes a flavored dark brown drink. But did you know that the same procedures can be used to produce colored solutions from other natural substances?

The skins and innards of many fruits and vegetables are strongly colored. Sometimes the juice can stain your clothes. Which fruits and vegetables are strong enough to color water? In this activity you'll find out.

You will need:

    1 piece of broomstick or dowel, 6 inches long and 1 inch in diameter

    kitchen knife

    potato peeler

    clean glass jar

    tin can

    package of cone coffee filter paper (No. 2 size)

    metal or heat-resistant plastic funnel (the top must be large enough
        to sit on the jar)

    medium-size saucepan

    wooden spoon

    pot holder

    small glass jars, such as baby-food jars or ones of similar capacity

    water

    masking tape

For foods to test, you can use:

    blueberries

    strawberries

    carrots

    spinach

    oranges

    lemons

    beets

    red cabbage

Or try other fruits and vegetables and see what happens.

 SAFETY NOTE: This activity should be done with an adult.

Getting Started

Step 1.   Before coffee is made, the coffee beans must be ground, because particles release more flavor than a whole bean. For the same reason, in this activity the fruits and vegetables should be in small pieces, too. So, using the knife for a soft substance or the potato peeler for a hard one, cut one of the foods into small pieces.

Place these small pieces in the can. Then, mash these pieces with the dowel or broomstick until they form a mushy mixture.

Step 2.   Spoon the mashed food into the saucepan. Add just enough to cover the bottom. Then add just enough water to cover the food. (If you add too much water, it will take a long time to cook, and the color will be diluted.)

Have an adult turn on the stove. Let the solution boil uncovered for at least 5 minutes but try not to let the water boil away.

Step 3.   Put the funnel into the glass jar. Put a coffee filter inside the funnel.

COFFEE FILTER

FUNNEL

GLASS JAR OR
TIN CAN

Turn off the heat on the stove. Let the cooked solution cool a little. Then have an adult pour the liquid from the saucepan into the funnel. Let it drain through the filter into the jar.

Step 4.   When all the liquid has drained out, let the solution cool completely. Then pour it into one of the small jars, and use a piece of masking tape to label the jar with the name of the food and its color.

Experiments to Try

Following the steps on pages 17–18, repeat the experiment with different foods and try to answer these questions. (Make sure you wash the utensils between uses and use a new coffee filter.)

- If big chunks of a food are used, what color does the water become?
- If you cook the solution until it is almost gone, what color does the water become?
- Which fruits give the strongest color? Which ones give the weakest color?
- Which vegetables give the strongest, and which give the weakest, colors?
- Which solutions are clear? Which are cloudy?
- What happens to the color when you boil the filtered solution until most of the water is gone?

Save the filtered solutions. You will be using them for future experiments.

What's Happening?
You should have found that blueberries, beets, and red cabbage give very strongly colored solutions, whereas other foods, such as carrots, lemons, and oranges, do not. Mashing the fruit or vegetable into small pieces releases some of the liquid holding the color, and small pieces of cooked food break down and release their ingredients faster than large chunks of food do. Cooking the pieces longer generally produces more color, especially in the case of red cabbage, spinach, and carrots. The colored substance in food, called *pigment,* is dissolved in a liquid that is housed in a protective layer within the plant. The two techniques of mashing and cooking help release the pigment solution from this protective layer.

When the solution passes through the filter paper, it leaves behind most of the pulp, or solid material, of the fruit or vegetable. Sometimes there is still color in the pulp. This may be because the solution did not boil long enough to extract all the color. But there may be another reason, too: The pigments in different fruits and vegetables have different capacities for *dissolving,* or mixing, in the water. This capacity is called *solubility.* For instance, carrot pigment does not dissolve in water as readily as blueberry pigment, even though both raw foods are strongly colored.

When you filter the solution, both the water and the substance dissolved in the water pass through the paper. Everything else remains in the pulp. Therefore, filtering can be used to test whether different substances have actually dissolved in water or not. Some liquids appear to be cloudy because very fine particles are suspended, but not dissolved, in the liquid. Light will be blocked or dispersed by these particles. When these solutions are filtered, the suspended particles stay with the pulp, and generally the liquid is colorless. When the liquids are colored but not cloudy, this indicates that the pigment or pigments have mixed with the water. The pigment particles here are very, very small and pass through the holes of the filter paper.

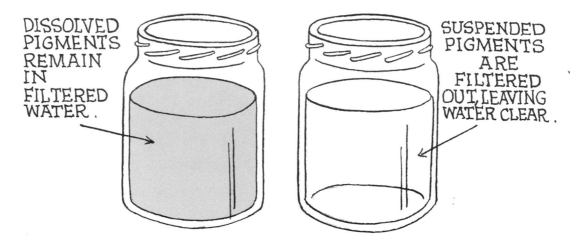

DISSOLVED PIGMENTS REMAIN IN FILTERED WATER.

SUSPENDED PIGMENTS ARE FILTERED OUT, LEAVING WATER CLEAR.

Boiling the liquid until it almost disappears concentrates whatever solid substances were originally in the solution. In some instances, this means that a colored solution will become darker.

You may have noticed that some of the filtered solutions have an aroma, or smell, even if they have very little color. This is most evident with oranges and lemons. It indicates that an aroma-causing substance can dissolve in water just as a pigment does. You will be experimenting with aroma in some of the next sections.

EXTRACTING NATURAL FLAVOR

One of the simplest and most common ways of extracting natural flavors is to cut food into pieces and then squeeze the chunks. The liquid that comes out has flavor, color, and aroma. Orange and lemon juices are prepared this way.

Other foods need to be cooked or to sit in warm or hot water before their flavor is released. This is the way vanilla flavoring is prepared. Vanilla flavoring comes from a bean, which has to be kept in hot water for a while to extract the flavor.

You can experiment with vanilla and other natural substances to see how well you are able to extract flavors from them. Since you will be tasting your results, make sure you use very clean equipment, and wash the food you are using before you begin, too.

You will need:
> the equipment from page 16
> lid that fits the saucepan
> set of measuring spoons
> metal ladle or large metal spoon
> graduated measuring cup
> drinking glasses

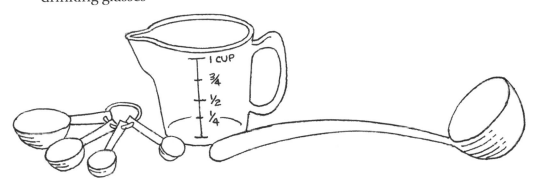

For foods to test, you can use:

    the fruits and vegetables from page 16

    ginger (This is available in the produce section of many supermarkets.)

    vanilla beans (These are available in the spice sections of most large
      supermarkets.)

    cinnamon sticks

    cloves

You can also try other spices that you think will give interesting results, but don't use ground spices—they have less flavor than whole spices do.

 SAFETY NOTE: This activity should be done with an adult.

Getting Started

To prepare the fruits and vegetables, follow Step 1 on page 17.

To prepare the spices, use the knife to chop them into small pieces. The cinnamon sticks can be broken and then pounded with the broomstick.

Experiments to Try

• Place about 2 tablespoons of one of the spices in the saucepan. Just barely cover the spices with water. Have an adult turn on the stove. Heat the solution until the water is boiling, then cover the pan and turn the heat down to a simmer. After 5 minutes, turn off the heat. Holding the handle of the pan with a pot holder, use the ladle or the large metal spoon to scoop out a tablespoonful of the hot solution after 5 minutes. Scoop out another sample after 10 minutes and another after 15 minutes. Filter each of these solutions into a separate clean drinking glass and label each of the glasses. Let them all cool completely. Then taste these solutions one at a time. Do they taste the same?

Repeat this procedure for all of the spices and kinds of food you want to test.

- Fill the saucepan with water and heat it to boiling. Turn off the heat. Holding the handle of the pan with a pot holder, use the ladle or the large metal spoon to scoop out some water. Measure $\frac{1}{4}$ cup of water and pour it into a glass. *Be careful not to burn yourself.* Put $\frac{1}{4}$ cup of hot water into a separate glass for each food you are experimenting with. Add 1 teaspoon of chopped food to each glass.

  Let the solutions sit for 15 minutes and then filter each of them.

  Compare the taste of these *hot-water-bath solutions* to the boiled solutions of the same food from the first experiment. Are they the same?

- Let the solutions you have collected sit uncovered at room temperature in a warm open area for a few days. Does anything remain in the glass after the liquid has evaporated?

What's Happening?

The process of extracting flavors is similar to extracting color, and the results are similar. The longer you cook a solution, the more flavor will be released. However, if some substances, such as the vanilla beans, are cooked too long, the flavor can actually become weaker. This is why cookbooks recommend that some ingredients be left to *steep,* or soak, in hot water rather than be boiled. This more gentle process releases the flavor but doesn't boil it off into the air.

One of the major differences between flavor and color is that flavor can evaporate. When a colored liquid is allowed to evaporate, the pigments, which are usually solids, remain in the container as a solid residue. However, when a flavored solution evaporates, the flavors, which are often volatile liquids, pass easily from a liquid to a gaseous state and evaporate with the water.

CONCENTRATING AROMAS

When cooking spices, their aroma is especially noticeable. Even after the spice solutions are passed through a filter, the aroma is strong, although it weakens fairly quickly. These observations suggest that the source of the aroma, which is called the food's *essence,* mixes with the water but is easily driven from the water by heat. This property of forming a gas easily from a liquid can be taken advantage of when extracting flavors and aromas using a special technique, called *distillation,* which captures the vapors coming off a boiling solution.

Distillation has been used for centuries and is still used in some manufacturing processes and chemical laboratories. You can easily put together a simple distillery, or still, in your kitchen.

You will need:
    1 medium-size metal pan that has a lid with a knob or handle in the center
    1 piece of heavy-duty aluminum foil, 12 inches long
    1 piece of flexible metal wire, 12–14 inches long
    nail
    set of measuring spoons
    water
    ice cubes
    pot holder
    grater
    knife
    small glass jars with lids

For foods to test, you can use:
    lemon peel
    orange peel

ground cinnamon

ground cloves

anise

ground nutmeg

vanilla beans

 SAFETY NOTE: This activity should be done with an adult.

Getting Started

Step 1.   Cut a sheet of aluminum foil so that it is 6 inches wide by 12 inches long.

Step 2.   Fold the foil as shown to make a 3-inch square.

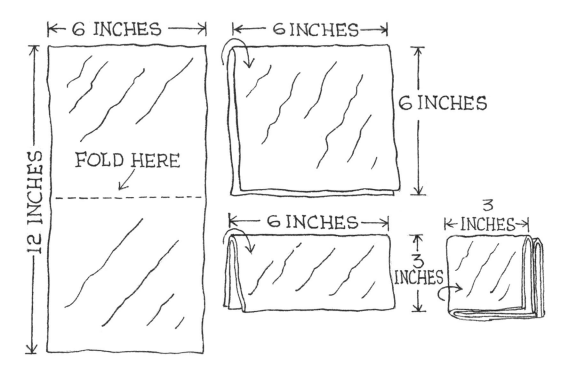

Step 3. Open the folded foil to form a cone-shaped cup.

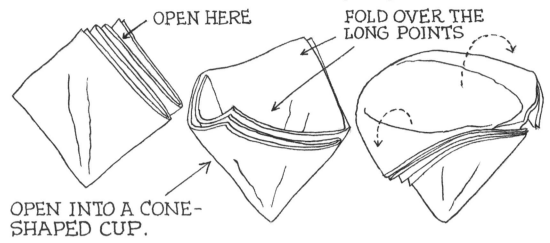

OPEN HERE

FOLD OVER THE
LONG POINTS

OPEN INTO A CONE-
SHAPED CUP.

Step 4. Use a nail to punch 2 holes directly opposite each other about $\frac{1}{2}$ inch below the rim of the cup.

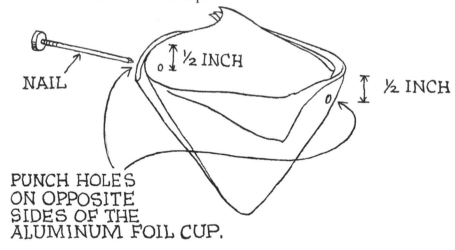

NAIL

½ INCH

½ INCH

PUNCH HOLES
ON OPPOSITE
SIDES OF THE
ALUMINUM FOIL CUP.

Step 5. Push the wire through the 2 holes in the cup. Twist the 2 ends of the wire around the knob of the pot lid. The cup should hang straight when the lid is upside down and level, and it should be close to, but not touching, the knob.

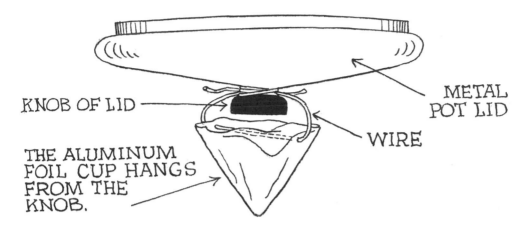

KNOB OF LID

METAL POT LID

WIRE

THE ALUMINUM FOIL CUP HANGS FROM THE KNOB.

Step 6. Place about 2 tablespoons of a spice in the bottom of the pan. Add enough hot tap water to cover the bottom.

Step 7. Put the pan on the stove and start heating it. When the water begins to boil, put the upside-down lid on the pan, with the hanging foil cup attached. Make sure that the cup is hanging freely directly below the knob and is not touching the boiling water below it.

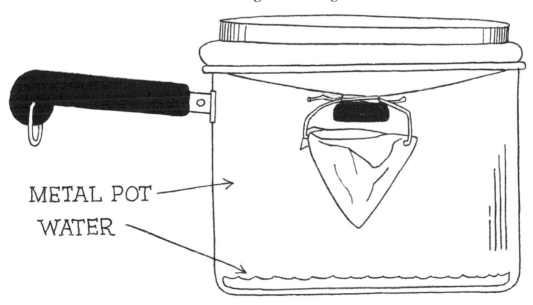

METAL POT

WATER

Step 8. Fill the lid with ice cubes and add water until the lid is half-filled.

Step 9. As the solution in the pan continues to boil, steam or vapor will form inside the pan. When the rising vapor touches the cold lid, it will form liquid droplets that combine with each other, roll down toward the center of the lid, and drop into the foil cup.

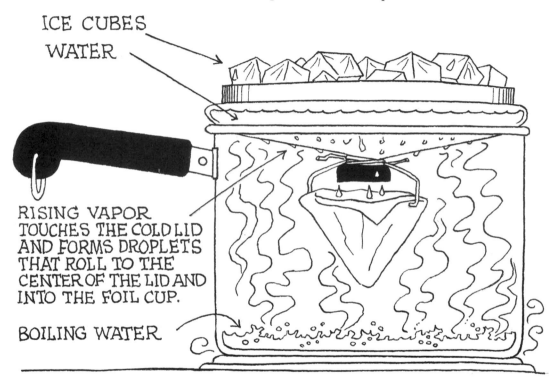

ICE CUBES

WATER

RISING VAPOR TOUCHES THE COLD LID AND FORMS DROPLETS THAT ROLL TO THE CENTER OF THE LID AND INTO THE FOIL CUP.

BOILING WATER

Using a pot holder, lift up the lid slightly every few minutes to see if there is liquid in the cup. *Make sure not to put your face too close to the lid, though, because hot steam will be escaping through the opening when you lift up the lid.* Also, check to see that there is still some solution in the bottom of the pan. If the solution is running low, add more water. When there is some liquid in the foil cup, ask an adult to pour the liquid from the cup into a glass jar while you hold the lid.

Step 10. As the liquid continues to accumulate in the cup, take 3 or 4 samples. Store each in a different jar, and label each in the order it was taken.

Step 11. Prepare other test materials. Use the grater to grate the orange or lemon peel; with the knife, chop the vanilla beans into small pieces the size of coarse grains of sand.

Then follow Steps 1 through 10 to test these and the other spices and fruits.

Experiments to Try

- Which spices give the strongest-smelling solution after distillation? Which give the weakest?
- How does the strength of the aroma from the first sample you collected compare to the last sample of the same material? (To double-check your results, have someone who has not been smelling the experiment as you performed it help you test this.)
- What happens if you don't put ice cubes or water inside the lid?
- Let the solutions you have collected sit uncovered at room temperature in a warm open area for a few days. What happens?

What's Happening?

All of the solutions that you collect from the cup should be clear and should have an aroma similar to the original natural ingredient. The first samples that you collect will be stronger than the later ones, and some foods will produce stronger smells than others. The solution from cloves tends to smell very strong, whereas ginger and cinnamon are weaker.

When water and the test materials are heated to boiling, they form a vapor or gas that circulates inside the pan. When the vapor hits the cool surface of the lid, it forms a liquid. Both of these actions are examples of what scientists call a *change of state,* or a *phase change.* Water and aroma forming a gas is one phase change. The vapor forming a liquid solution is another phase change.

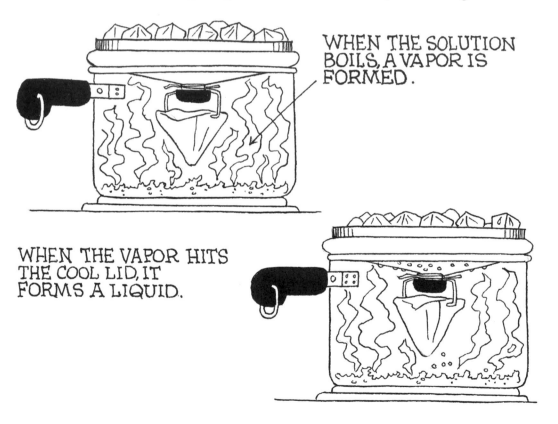

WHEN THE SOLUTION BOILS, A VAPOR IS FORMED.

WHEN THE VAPOR HITS THE COOL LID, IT FORMS A LIQUID.

In both instances, heat exchange is involved. To form the gas, heat had to be added to the liquid. To form the liquid, heat is removed by using it to melt the ice cubes and warm up the cool water in the lid. If the water in the lid gets too hot or if there is no ice or water at all, the gas will not form a liquid. Water is an example of a substance that can move through three phase changes. It can freeze to become ice, melt to become a liquid, and boil to evaporate and become a gas.

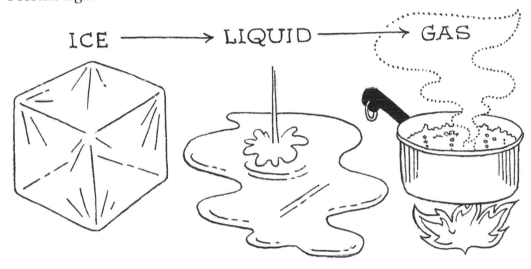

ICE ⟶ LIQUID ⟶ GAS

There is an important difference between the aroma and the color obtained. As you have seen from one of your previous activities, if you let a colored solution sit around for several days to evaporate, a colored solid substance will remain on the bottom of the cup. However, if you let an aromatic solution sit around until it evaporates, there will be nothing remaining at the bottom of the cup. This demonstrates that the aroma-producing substance that was dissolved in the water was a liquid that turned into a gas. It also shows that other liquids can evaporate, as water can. The fact that you can easily smell some of the aromas is an indicator that they readily go into the air.

Making a Different Kind of Still

Instead of using a saucepan and lid, you can make a still using other simple materials.

You will need:

    2 large empty canned-tomato cans, one can with both ends removed
    1 metal (not plastic) funnel, about 4 inches in diameter at the top
    1 cork with a diameter just large enough to fit into the hole of the funnel
    1 package of oil-based clay, such as Plasticine
    duct tape
    1 piece of heavy-duty aluminum foil, 12 inches long
    1 piece of flexible metal wire, 12–14 inches long
    knife
    hammer
    nail, 2 inches long

Step 1.   Tape the 2 cans together with duct tape, as shown in the drawing.

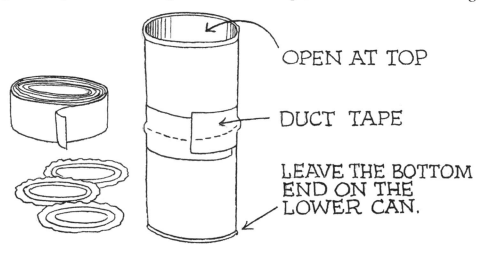

OPEN AT TOP

DUCT TAPE

LEAVE THE BOTTOM END ON THE LOWER CAN.

Step 2.   Taper one end of the cork with the knife so that it fits snugly inside the hole of the funnel.

CUT THE SIDES OF THE CORK A LITTLE SO IT FITS SNUGLY IN THE NECK OF THE FUNNEL.

Step 3.   Fill in any gaps between the funnel and the cork with Plasticine. Some metal funnels have a seam down the side. If yours does, cover this seam with Plasticine also so that no water will leak from it.

Step 4.   Follow Steps 1 through 4 on pages 25–26 to make the aluminum-foil cup.

Step 5.   With the hammer and the nail, punch holes in the bottom of the funnel below the cork, as shown.

CORK

PUNCH HOLES ON OPPOSITE SIDES OF THE FUNNEL.

Step 6. Push the wire through the 2 holes in the funnel and then through the 2 holes in the cup. The cup should hang freely just below the tip of the funnel. Twist the 2 ends of the wire together to hold the cup in place.

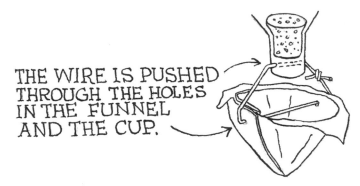

THE WIRE IS PUSHED
THROUGH THE HOLES
IN THE FUNNEL
AND THE CUP.

Step 7. In this still, the 2 cans take the place of the pan, and the funnel functions as the lid.

Continuing from Step 6 on page 27, carry out the experiment. *Be very careful not to burn yourself or tip over the apparatus.*

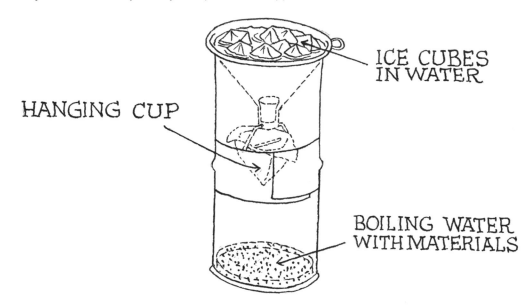

ICE CUBES
IN WATER

HANGING CUP

BOILING WATER
WITH MATERIALS

EXAMINING SPOILAGE

As you probably already know, fruits and vegetables rot or spoil when left at room temperature. They last longer in the refrigerator, but eventually they will spoil in there, too. Some of your solutions from the previous activity have fruits or vegetables in them. Does this mean they will spoil, even if they have been cooked? Using the solutions you made in the previous activities, you can see if cooking makes a difference.

You will need:
    the filtered, boiled solutions from pages 16–19
    1 package of clear plastic wine cups
    1 package of clear plastic wrap
    labels
    set of measuring spoons
    salt
    lemon juice

Getting Started

Step 1.   Select 3 or 4 of the solutions you prepared previously.

Step 2.   Pour some of the first solution into 5 cups, to a depth of about $\frac{1}{2}$ inch. Label each cup 1 through 5, and add the name of the solution. Then put the following information on the labels:

for Cup 1: Refrigerated
for Cup 2: Warm Spot
for Cup 3: Room Temperature
for Cup 4: Salt Added
for Cup 5: Covered

Step 3.   To the solution in Cup 4, add 1 teaspoon of salt. Cover Cup 5 with plastic wrap.

Step 4.   Repeat Steps 2 and 3 for each solution you want to test.

Step 5.   You can also compare freshly squeezed lemon juice to cooked lemon juice. Line up two sets of 5 cups, as before, for the 5 different conditions. In one set of cups, put 1 tablespoon of the fresh lemon juice. In the other set, put 1 tablespoon of the cooked lemon juice. Label the cups.

Step 6.   Put all the cups labeled Refrigerated into the refrigerator. Put all the cups labeled Room Temperature in an out-of-the-way place where they won't be tipped over. Put the Warm Spot and Salt Added cups near a heater, radiator, or sunny window.

Step 7.   Check all the cups every day, and record what you find.

Step 8.   After 7 days, compare the sets.

Experiments to Try

- Does the temperature affect the rate of spoilage for some or all of the solutions? (Make sure you compare only Cups 1, 2, and 3, where the only difference is temperature.)
- Compare Cup 3 and Cup 5 for each solution. Does covering a cup affect the rate of spoilage?
- Compare Cup 2 and Cup 4 for each solution. What effect does salt have on spoilage?
- Compare all the cups containing the same original solution. Which spoiled fastest? Which lasted the longest?
- Which of your test solutions spoiled first? Which spoiled last?
- Compare the solution containing the freshly squeezed lemon juice to the one containing the cooked lemon juice. Which one spoiled more quickly?

What's Happening?

After a few days, you will start to see growth of molds on the top of some of the solutions kept at room temperature. For those solutions kept in the warm places, this growth will be greater and faster. The solutions stored in the refrigerator will keep longer. Salt added to solutions will also slow down the rate of spoilage. Uncovered cups will spoil faster than covered ones. Fresh and cooked lemon juice may give different results compared with the other solutions because lemon juice is naturally acidic—that's why it has a tart taste. Acid conditions can sometimes slow down the rate at which the solution spoils.

Spoilage occurs because bacteria and molds were in the air or in the cups or were trapped in the solution during handling. Heat speeds up their multiplication. Adding chemicals such as salt will slow down their growth. This is why you should close containers of food and place them in the refrigerator if you don't finish them at one sitting and wish to eat or drink more later. Some manufacturers add chemicals to retard the growth of bacteria.

When the makers of soda are preparing the solutions at the factory, they are supposed to take care that the bottles have been thoroughly cleaned. The ingredients are cooked or steamed to destroy bacteria. Once the bottles are sealed, the solution is safe for a while, but even those with added chemical retardants will spoil eventually. This is why some bottles have dates stamped on their labels to indicate how long the sodas will remain fresh.

ADDING FIZZ

You have probably seen the term *carbonated water* on soda bottle labels. This means that carbon dioxide has been dissolved in water. It is this gas that makes the bubbling and the fizzing you see when a bottle or can of soda is opened. These characteristics are so strongly associated with drinking soda that most people feel it isn't soda if it doesn't fizz.

Before the sodas that we drink today were created, there was another kind of special liquid that was bottled and drunk by people. These were waters that came from natural springs. People drank these liquids because they thought they would cure different kinds of sicknesses.

One kind of natural springwater has bubbles. Some scientists experimented to make a similar kind of water from chemicals. Around 1770, Joseph Priestley, an English scientist, was one of the first to make a bubbly solution. Some of these bubbly liquids continue to be used as medicine, while others were transformed into popular soft drinks.

There are several ways that you can make a fizzy solution that contains carbon dioxide. One of them involves using a living organism called yeast. Another way is to use an ordinary chemical that releases gas when mixed with certain kinds of liquids. These substances are probably already in your kitchen. With a few additional pieces of equipment, you can experiment with them and see how gas can be generated and how it mixes with water. These two methods generate gas in the solution, where it mixes with the water. A third way is to bubble the gas through the water and allow it to dissolve.

This chapter shows you how to try out all three methods.

MAKING SODA GAS WITH YEAST

When certain fruits and vegetables are mixed with water and allowed to sit for several days, a gas forms in the mixture. You saw this happen when you allowed your cooked solutions to sit for several days. If you closely observed the results of your experiments in the previous section, you could see some bubbling occurring or some foam at the top of the liquids. The gas causing this is produced by living organisms that are on the fruits and vegetables. Centuries ago people learned how to control this action and make different kinds of fizzy drinks.

You can use yeast, which is a living organism, to see what materials and conditions produce this gas.

You will need:
    several 1-liter plastic soda bottles with caps (They should be cleaned very
       thoroughly.)
    set of measuring spoons
    1 package of round balloons, at least 9 inches in diameter

several packages of dry yeast

sugar

maple or clear Karo syrup

honey

molasses

1 package of artificial sweetener (such as aspartame)

water

small funnel

Getting Started

Step 1. Use the funnel to put 5 teaspoons of sugar and 1 package of yeast in a soda bottle.

Step 2. Add warm water to the bottle until it is about half full. Swirl the solution around until the sugar is dissolved.

Step 3. Fill the bottle with more warm water until the level of the liquid is about 1 inch below the rim of the bottle.

Step 4. Screw the cap on tightly, but not so tightly that it will be difficult to take off.

Step 5. Let the bottle sit undisturbed at room temperature for about half an hour. Then shake the contents. Slowly twist the cap and listen. Do you hear any hissing sound? Twist the cap on tightly and let the bottle sit for a day.

Note Carefully: *The generated gas will build up pressure in the bottle. The bottle will become hard—similar to a regular unopened soda bottle. However, care should be taken when opening these bottles. There can be a great deal of spraying. It is advised that you place a towel over the cap of the bottle when untwisting the cap.*

Experiments to Try

- Follow Steps 1 through 3 on page 43, but do not cap or shake the bottle. Observe the bottle occasionally over several days, and record when the gas no longer is being generated.
- Fill a bottle with water and add 5 teaspoons of sugar. Fill another bottle, and add 1 package of yeast. Tightly cap each bottle. Check every day to see if any gas has been generated. The bottle will feel hard if there is lots of gas. Another way to check is to slowly untwist the cap and listen for a hissing sound, which is the sound of escaping gas.
- Set up 3 clean bottles. To the first add 5 teaspoons of sugar, to the second add 10 teaspoons of sugar, to the third add 15 teaspoons of sugar. Add 1 package of yeast to each bottle. Fill each with warm water to 1 inch below the rim. Cap the bottles tightly and shake well. Check the bottles every day. Does increasing the sugar generate more gas? Does it make the bubbling last longer?
- Set up 3 clean bottles. Add 5 teaspoons of sugar to each. Add 1 package of yeast to the first bottle, 2 packages of yeast to the second bottle, and 3 packages of yeast to the third. Fill the bottles with warm water to 1 inch below the rim. Cap the bottles and shake well. Check them every day. Does increasing the yeast generate more gas? Does it make the bubbling last longer?
- Set up 3 clean bottles. In the first, put 5 teaspoons of maple or Karo syrup. In the second, put 5 teaspoons of honey. In the third, put 5 teaspoons of molasses. Add 1 package of yeast to each. Fill the bottles with warm water to 1 inch below the rim. Cap the bottles and shake well. Check them every day. How does the gas generation here compare with the earlier experiment that combined 5 teaspoons of sugar and 1 package of yeast?
- As in the previous experiments, put 5 teaspoons of sugar, 1 package of yeast,

and warm water in a clean bottle. Instead of sealing it with the cap, place a large round balloon securely around the neck of the bottle. Check the balloon occasionally to see how much it is inflated. How large does the balloon become? How long does it stay inflated?

• Put 10 teaspoons of artificial sweetener, 1 package of yeast, and warm water in a clean bottle. Will this also generate gas?

What's Happening?
The combination of yeast and sugar produces gas in the solution. As more gas is produced, the flexible plastic of the bottle becomes hard. This tells you that the pressure inside has become very high. If you slowly open the cap after one day, gas and some of the solution come rushing out. This spraying can last for several seconds, indicating that a lot of gas was

produced. If you shake the bottle, even more gas and solution will come rushing out. The solution foams up very easily, resulting in lots of it spilling out of the bottle.

If you recap the bottle containing the remaining solution and untwist the cap again the next day, you may get more foaming and more gas released. That means the gas-producing process is continuing. If the solution doesn't fizz, the process has ended.

An important question to ask yourself is whether the gas is coming from the yeast, from the sugar, or from a combination of both. One of the experiments you did can help answer this question. Putting yeast and sugar in separate bottles of water does not produce gas. You need a combination of yeast and sugar. The yeast is a microorganism that uses sugar as a food. It eats the sugar. This process, called *fermentation*, produces carbon dioxide, the gas that makes the fizz, and other chemicals. The more food, or sugar, you add, the more gas and chemicals are produced. Eventually these products of fermentation kill off the yeast, and the process stops.

What happens if you add more and more yeast to a solution without adding more and more sugar? The amount of gas produced depends on the amount of food available. Once all the sugar has been eaten, the yeast microorganisms no longer have any food, so they can no longer multiply; therefore no more gas is produced. This indicates that there is a point where adding more yeast will not generate more gas.

Yeast will act on other types of sweet substances, as you saw in your experiments with the honey, molasses, and syrups. These all contain ingredients from the family of substances called sugars. Different sugars have different names, such as glucose, fructose, and dextrose. Gas is produced when yeast is mixed with honey, molasses, or syrup in water, but it will be produced more slowly than in a regular sugar and yeast mix. Yeast mixed with artificial sweeteners, such as NutraSweet, also produces gas, but not as quickly or as abundantly as yeast mixed with regular sugar. Yeast will not act on all sweet substances, but it will act on most of the sweeteners found in the average kitchen.

If a bottle containing a mixture of yeast and sugars is uncapped, no pressure builds up in the bottle, since the gas is escaping all the time. However, if you put your finger over the opening and shake the bottle vigorously, you will feel pressure. When you slowly release your finger, you can hear a slight hissing sound and see foaming. This indicates that some of the gas that was dissolved in the water is now escaping into the air.

The opposite process occurs in the manufacturing of sodas. Yeast is not used to put the gas into the soda solution. Instead, the gases go into the solution when the gases and the liquid are placed under high pressure.

MAKING SODA GAS WITH CHEMICALS

This is a quicker and more direct way of introducing gas into a soda solution than by using yeast. The ingredients for experimenting with this process are already in your kitchen. All you need are different kinds of fruit juices and some baking soda.

You will need:
    1 package of clear plastic cups, 9-ounce size
    set of measuring spoons
    1 package of round balloons, at least 9 inches in diameter
    several clean 1-liter soda bottles with caps (They should be cleaned very
       thoroughly.)
    small funnel
    spoon
    water
    baking soda
    baking powder
    sugar

For juices to test, you can use:
    orange juice
    lemon juice

apple juice

cranberry juice

You can also try other fruit juices that you think will give interesting results.

Getting Started

Step 1. Measure out 1 teaspoon of baking soda into a clear plastic cup. Add 5 tablespoons of water and stir thoroughly.

Step 2. Measure out 1 tablespoon of one of the juices into the same cup. Stir thoroughly. Watch closely to see what happens.

Step 3. Record the results in your notebook.

Experiments to Try

• Follow Steps 1 through 3 above, and test all your juices. Which juices fizz when they are added to the baking-soda solution? Which ones don't? Keep a record, and save the solutions that fizzed for the next experiment.

• To one of the solutions that fizzed, add 1 *teaspoon* of the same juice. Keep adding 1 teaspoon of juice at a time until there is no longer any fizzing. How much juice do you have to add before the fizzing stops? Carry out the same procedure with the other solutions that fizzed. And don't forget to record your results.

• Follow Steps 1 through 3 above, but substitute baking powder for baking soda. Do you get the same results?

• Measure out 5 tablespoons of water into a clear plastic cup. Add 1 teaspoon of baking powder. What happens?

- Follow Steps 1 through 3 on page 49, but substitute sugar for the baking soda or baking powder. Do any of the juices fizz?
- Put a balloon over the neck of the funnel. Pour 5 teaspoons of baking powder into the funnel, let it slide into the balloon, and take the balloon off the funnel.

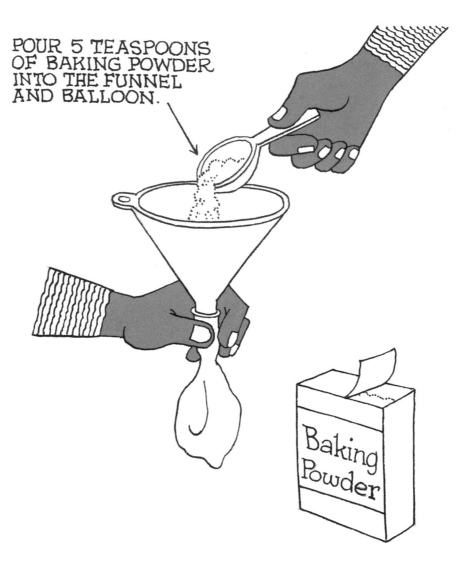

POUR 5 TEASPOONS OF BAKING POWDER INTO THE FUNNEL AND BALLOON.

Baking Powder

Then measure 5 teaspoons of lemon juice into a 1-liter soda bottle.

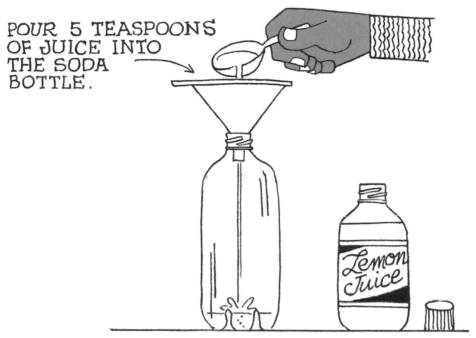

POUR 5 TEASPOONS OF JUICE INTO THE SODA BOTTLE.

Carefully slide the neck of the balloon over the neck of the bottle. Shake the balloon so that the baking powder falls into the lemon juice. Shake the bottle so that the two substances mix thoroughly. What happens to the balloon?

- Repeat the previous experiment, but substitute apple juice or cranberry juice for lemon juice. What happens to the balloon?
- Repeat the experiment, but vary the amount of baking soda or the amount of juice. How does this affect the result?

What's Happening?
Baking soda is the common name for sodium bicarbonate. When you add lemon juice to baking soda and water, you will produce a very fizzy solution. Orange juice will produce some fizzing, but not as much as the lemon juice.

Apple juice and cranberry juice will not produce any fizzing, although you may see a few small bubbles.

When you substitute baking powder for baking soda, all of the juices produce fizzing. In fact, baking powder and water alone will fizz, even with no juice added. This is because baking powder is baking soda with added ingredients. These added ingredients act in the same way as the lemon juice and orange juice. When they mix with water, they form substances called *acids*, and acids all react with baking soda to produce a gas. You need the combination of acid, sodium bicarbonate, and water to produce fizzing. Apple and cranberry juice give very weak reactions with baking soda because they contain very weak acids. Depending on the kind of acids in the juice, you will get a range of reactions with baking soda.

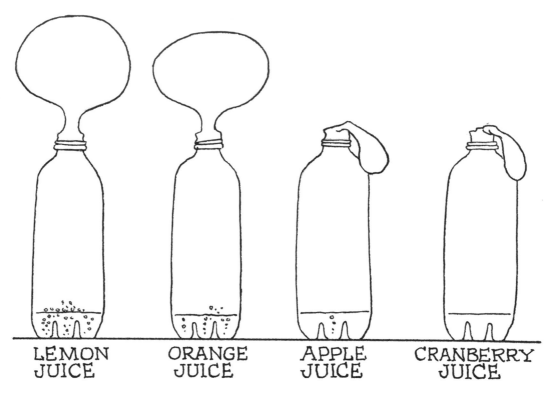

LEMON
JUICE

ORANGE
JUICE

APPLE
JUICE

CRANBERRY
JUICE

If you keep adding teaspoonfuls of juice to a solution that already fizzes, there is a point where the extra juice no longer results in more fizzing. This is because all of the sodium bicarbonate has been changed by the reaction and so is no longer affected by the extra acid. Part of the sodium bicarbonate has been converted into the gas carbon dioxide, which is the gas that makes the fizz, and the rest has been changed into another substance that remains in the solution.

If you add lemon juice or orange juice to sugar and water, there is no fizz. This is also true if you use a different sweetener. Sugar substances do not contain sodium bicarbonate, and sodium bicarbonate is necessary to produce the gas that makes the fizz.

When you mix lemon juice or orange juice with baking soda in a bottle and attach a balloon to the neck, the balloon will inflate. The more of these ingredients you use, the more the balloon will expand. This shows that the fizzing action is the escaping of the gas carbon dioxide. You can't see the gas, but you can observe its effects. When you use apple juice or cranberry juice in this arrangement, the balloon doesn't inflate. This confirms your observation from the previous experiments: Those juices did not fizz when they were added to the baking-soda solution; therefore, no gas was being produced.

When you vary the amounts of the ingredients, the size of the balloon does not change much. If you use a lot of baking soda and not much juice, there is baking soda left over in the solution after the gas is produced. If you add lots of juice and not much baking soda, there is juice left over. This shows that the proportions of these two ingredients have to be just right for both to be used up during the reaction.

You can now see that there is one big problem in using baking soda to make a fizzy soda. You won't be able to use some popular juices and flavors, like apple or cranberry juice, because they won't fizz. Another problem is that you will have to be very careful how much of each ingredient you use. If you use too much baking soda, it will be left over in the solution, and its taste will be noticeable.

In the next section, you will experiment with another way of making fizz that doesn't have these undesirable side effects.

DISSOLVING SODA GAS IN WATER

In the fermentation experiments in the previous section, you saw that both yeast and sodium bicarbonate will produce gas but that there are drawbacks to both if you want a drinkable soda. However, there is another way to make a fizzy solution. You can dissolve the gas in water by itself. This section shows you how to do this.

You will need:
    1 piece of plastic tubing, 3 feet long by $\frac{1}{4}$ inch in diameter (This is
        available at most hardware stores or aquarium supply stores.)
    1 package of round balloons, at least 9 inches in diameter
    two 2-liter plastic soda bottles (They should be cleaned very thoroughly.)

rubber bands
large bucket
small funnel
set of measuring spoons
scissors
baking soda
baking powder
vinegar
lemon juice
different types of fruit juices
water

Getting Started

Step 1. Fill a large bucket $\frac{3}{4}$ full with water. Fill a 2-liter plastic soda bottle with water. Cover the opening of the bottle with your hand, turn the bottle over, and set it into the bucket of water.

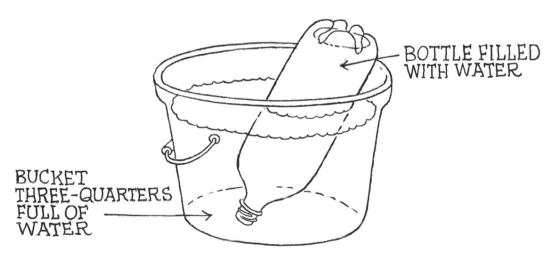

BOTTLE FILLED WITH WATER

BUCKET THREE-QUARTERS FULL OF WATER

Step 2. Pour 4 tablespoons of vinegar or lemon juice into the other 2-liter bottle.

Step 3. Cut the bottom end of a round balloon.

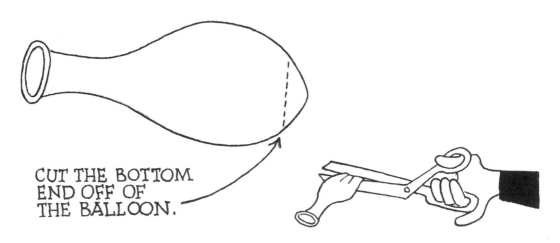

CUT THE BOTTOM
END OFF OF
THE BALLOON.

Slide the cut end onto one end of the piece of plastic tubing. Wrap a rubber band around the balloon to hold it tightly to the tubing.

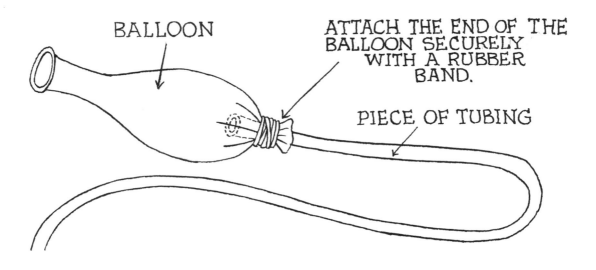

BALLOON

ATTACH THE END OF THE
BALLOON SECURELY
WITH A RUBBER
BAND.

PIECE OF TUBING

Step 4.   Pour 2 tablespoons of baking soda into the neck of the balloon. Try to keep the baking soda in the balloon section and not let it fall into the plastic tubing.

Step 5.   Slide the free end of the plastic tubing into the neck of the upside-down bottle in the bucket. Then carefully place the neck of the balloon over the bottle containing the vinegar or lemon juice.

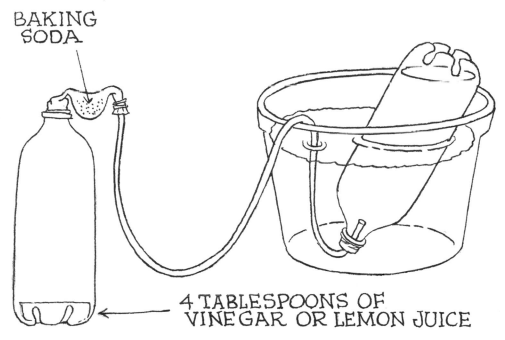

BAKING SODA

4 TABLESPOONS OF VINEGAR OR LEMON JUICE

Step 6.   Shake the balloon so that the baking soda falls into the bottle with the vinegar or lemon juice. This will cause the vinegar or lemon juice to fizz and produce a gas. The gas will travel along the tubing and into the upside-down bottle of water.

Let the bubbling continue until almost all of the water is out of the upside-down bottle. As the gas travels along the tubing and into the upside-down bottle of water, it pushes water out of the bottle. You can see the gas bubbles coming up to the top of the upside-down bottle. As this occurs, the top part of the bottle will appear empty. It is filled with the transparent gas.

Step 7.   Do not let the upside-down bottle containing the gas tip over. Place a rubber band on the bottle at the point where the water level is. Let the bottle sit for half an hour, then check it. There will be a change in the water level. Compare the new water level to the old one marked by the rubber band.

Experiments to Try

• As you did in the previous experiments, try different kinds of juices and see if the gas that is generated dissolves in the water.

• You can also substitute baking powder for baking soda and see if the gas dissolves in the water.

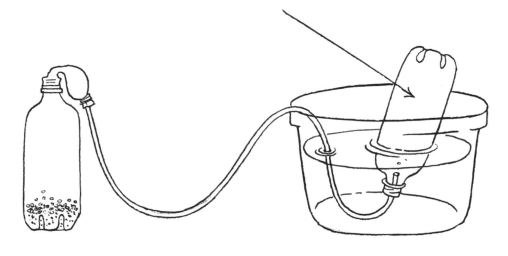

THE WATER IN THE BOTTLE
HAS BEEN DISPLACED
BY THE GAS.

What's Happening?

When gas is generated from the reaction of the acid and the vinegar, it bubbles into the bottle full of water, causing water to be displaced. This space in the bottle may look empty, but it does have carbon dioxide in it.

However, if you wait long enough, you will be able to see the water level rise again in the gas-filled bottle. There won't be enough water returning to fill up the whole bottle, but there will be a noticeable difference. This happens because some of the carbon dioxide gas dissolves in the water, so more water can come into the bottle to replace the volume of gas that dissolved.

The gas generated by vinegar, lemon juice, or any acidic juice will dissolve in water whether you use baking soda or baking powder. This is because all these combinations produce the same gas—carbon dioxide.

This process is similar to what happens at a soda bottling plant. The gas under high pressure is added to the beverage, and then the bottles are capped to prevent the gas from escaping and to maintain the pressure.

DESIGNING YOUR OWN SODA

The first sodas were made by pharmacists in drugstores more than a hundred years ago. They mixed different combinations of flavors in *carbonated water* (water that has dissolved carbon dioxide in it), creating their own special brands. Some of the earliest sodas were made with fruit flavors such as orange and lemon juice, but by 1890 sodas became so popular that a variety of artificial flavors were available. These could be mixed in different combinations for each individual customer. Some of the sodas mixed by a few pharmacists became very popular in their local cities. This was true for both Coca-Cola and Pepsi-Cola. With the development of special bottles and equipment, these sodas began to be distributed nationally.

The previous activities gave you the opportunity to find out about the specific characteristics of soft drinks. They showed how the different ingredients can be isolated from natural materials and, in some cases, how they can be concentrated. The next step is to combine these different ingredients and invent your own recipe. Now you, too, can become a designer of sodas!

INVENTING A RECIPE

The ingredients for making up your own special testing soda are already available in your kitchen or the nearest supermarket. Beyond that, all it takes is a good imagination and a willingness to experiment. You can try out all kinds of combinations of flavors and varying amounts of sugar to see what combination appeals to you the most.

You will need:
> 1 package of clear plastic cups, 9-ounce size (These should be thoroughly washed and rinsed after each experiment.)
> set of measuring spoons
> metric measuring cup
> spoon
> eyedropper
> water
> sugar
> baking soda
> 2 or 3 bottles of seltzer water
> 1 box of food color (This is usually available in the spice section of most supermarkets.)

For flavors to try out, you can start with lemon juice and orange juice, but you don't have to limit yourself to these. In the baking and spice section of your supermarket, you will find many concentrated flavors you can try, such as vanilla, mint, and peppermint.

Getting Started

There are a number of different ways that you can go about making up your own recipe and arriving at a good-tasting soda. The first thing you should do, though, is to decide what flavor you like the best. For instance, you may like lemon juice squeezed from fresh lemons or concentrated lemon juice that comes in a bottle. You can also use combinations of flavors.

Next, you need to decide how strong the flavor should be and how sweet or tart you want your soda to taste. You can control flavor strength and degree of sweetness by the amount of flavor and sugar you add to your solution. If you want the drink to fizz like a real soda, you can add baking soda or start with soda water. Finally, you can give your soda a color to make it look more appealing.

Experiments to Try

The following methods give you four different ways to design your own sodas systematically. You can try all four methods or just start with one as you try different flavors.

METHOD 1

Step 1. Measure out 100 milliliters of water, and pour it into a clean, clear plastic cup.

Step 2. Add 1, 2, or more teaspoons of the flavor that you have chosen. (If you are using concentrated flavors, use the eyedropper and add only 2 or 3 drops.)

Step 3. Add 1 or more teaspoons of sugar. Stir thoroughly.

Step 4. Place a few drops of your choice of food color in the solution.

Step 5. Taste. Then add more of any ingredient if this initial mix doesn't taste right to you. Keep track of how much of each ingredient you have added.

METHOD 2

Follow Steps 1 through 5 from Method 1 with any of the flavors. Then add baking soda to the solution to make it fizz. (Remember, though, that you will only get fizzing if you use lemon or orange juice.)

METHOD 3

Step 1. Measure out 100 milliliters of seltzer water.
Then follow Steps 1 through 5 from Method 1 with any of the flavors.

METHOD 4

This is a more systematic approach to determining what quantities of each ingredient give the best combination for a good-tasting soda.

Step 1. Fill 5 different cups with 100 milliliters of water or seltzer water each.

Step 2. To the first cup, add 1 teaspoon of fresh or concentrated flavoring;

to the second cup, add 2 teaspoons of flavoring; to the third cup, add 3 teaspoons of flavoring; to the fourth cup, add 4 teaspoons of flavoring; and to the fifth cup, add 5 teaspoons of flavoring.

Step 3. Add 1 teaspoon of sugar to each cup and stir.

Step 4. Taste each solution, and keep a record of the recipe that tastes best.

Step 5. Repeat Steps 1 and 2 using 5 clean cups and fresh water or seltzer.

Step 6. Add 2 teaspoons of sugar to each cup and stir.

Step 7. Taste and decide if you have found the right proportion of flavor and sweetness. If not, repeat Steps 1 and 2, and add 3 teaspoons of sugar to each cup.

Using this method you can systematically change the amount of flavor and sweetness and narrow down what are the best proportions of each. You can go back and forth tasting the solutions that have different proportions. You can also follow the same procedure to determine how much food color to add and, if you start with plain water, how much baking soda. If you are using seltzer water, carbonation is already present, so you don't need to add the baking powder or baking soda.

What's Happening?

The process that you use to invent your own soda is similar to the way that manufacturers make up new flavors. They also have to determine the best combination of ingredients and how much of each one to use. As you test your different recipes, it should become clear that the amount of each ingredient is very important, as is the proportion of the ingredients. For example, if you have a solution of 6 or 8 teaspoons of lemon juice and only 1 teaspoon of sugar, the taste will be sour. On the other hand, if you have 8 teaspoons of sugar and only 1 or 2 teaspoons of lemon juice, the taste will be too sweet. If you add 5 or 6 teaspoons of baking soda to the 100 milliliters of water, the baking soda taste will be too strong.

You also need to determine how much of each ingredient to add to 100 milliliters of water. For instance, 1 or 2 drops of red food color in 100 milliliters of water may be just right; 10 drops may be too dark to look appealing.

Keeping records of what you add and paying attention to the relative quantities are important for another reason. If you want to make larger amounts of your recipe, the ingredients should be in the same relative quantities as in the smaller batch. In this set of experiments, you start off each time with 100 milliliters for a special reason. Suppose you want to make a large batch of soda that is about 1 liter in volume? Since 1 liter is 1,000 milliliters, you multiply each of the ingredients you have in your original recipe by 10. (Ten times the 100 milliliters will give you 1 liter of water.) When you add the flavor and sugar, your batch will measure *slightly* more than 1 liter, but the relative proportions of the ingredients will be the same.

TESTING YOUR RECIPE ON OTHER PEOPLE

The recipe that you invent may be one that you like very much, but it may not be the right combination for most other people. People have different tastes for flavors and sweetness. To find out if others like the soda you design, you can conduct a survey, just as the food industry does with new products. Companies that make sodas seek out many people, ask them to taste their sodas, and also ask how their sodas can be improved.

You could ask family members and friends to taste and comment on your soda. This will give you some idea of how well your soda will be received. To get a better idea of whether your soda might sell well, you need to survey a larger number of people. For instance, you can have your classmates at school, or even the whole school, try your soda.

If you are going to ask more than a few people, you need to think of a way of conducting your survey. This section gives you some suggestions.

Designing the Survey

When conducting a survey, the first thing you need to do is decide what you want people to comment on.

- Do you want them only to indicate whether they like the soda or not?
- Do you want them to say something about the soda's different characteristics: flavor, sweetness, color, and fizziness?
- Do you want them to respond using a scale that would indicate how much they like or dislike each of the characteristics?

Each of these questions suggests the need for a different kind of survey. The first question gives you a little information and can be done quickly. The last question gives much more information, but the survey will take longer to do. You need to decide how much time you can give to the project and how much information you want to collect.

Here are some types of surveys that people have used.

METHOD A

The simplest type of survey is to let people taste a small amount of the soda and say whether they like it or not.

PEOPLE	1	2	3	4	5	6	7	8	9	10	11	12	13
LIKE													
DON'T LIKE													

This approach gives you a quick response and allows you to test many people. The results are easy to gather.

METHOD B

The next type of survey asks people to tell you whether they like the separate characteristics: flavor, sweetness, color, and fizz.

	PEOPLE	1	2	3	4	5	6	7	8	9	10
FLAVOR	LIKE										
	DON'T LIKE										
SWEETNESS	LIKE										
	DON'T LIKE										
COLOR	LIKE										
	DON'T LIKE										
FIZZ	LIKE										
	DON'T LIKE										

This approach provides more information and a better idea of what characteristics people like or don't like. Since asking more questions takes more time with each person, this kind of survey will take longer to conduct. But, like Method A, the results are easy to gather and study.

METHOD C

A third type of survey that gives you even more information can be used.

After they taste the soda, ask people to rank their reactions to the different characteristics, grading each from 1 to 10. They can give positive or negative responses for each of the characteristics by placing a check mark in the square under the number they think is appropriate for each characteristic.

	1	2	3	4	5	6	7	8	9	10
FLAVOR										
DON'T LIKE										LIKE
	1	2	3	4	5	6	7	8	9	10
SWEETNESS										
DON'T LIKE										LIKE
	1	2	3	4	5	6	7	8	9	10
COLOR										
DON'T LIKE										LIKE
	1	2	3	4	5	6	7	8	9	10
FIZZ										
DON'T LIKE										LIKE

This kind of survey will take more time to conduct, and when you gather and record the results, the chart is more complicated to study. But this method gives you very useful information. It can help you determine how you need to change the ingredients in your recipe to appeal to the most people.

Conducting the Survey

In order to conduct your survey, you need to find a place where you will encounter many people at the same time. Your classmates are one group of people you can draw upon. You could set up a table in the school cafeteria and have your schoolmates sample your soda and then respond to the survey. (Before you do this, however, you should get permission from your classroom teacher and the school principal.) You could also conduct your survey at a nearby shopping center, again getting permission from the manager of the center first.

Displaying Your Results

Once you have obtained enough responses, you should collect all the forms and add up the numbers.

To help you make sense of your results and also to show them to other people, you can make a graph. This is a special kind of picture showing all your results at once. It allows you to make comparisons very quickly.

Here are the results of a flavor survey. You can easily see that three people ranked the soda's flavor as a 2, fifteen people ranked it a 7, ten ranked it an 8, and five ranked it as a 10.

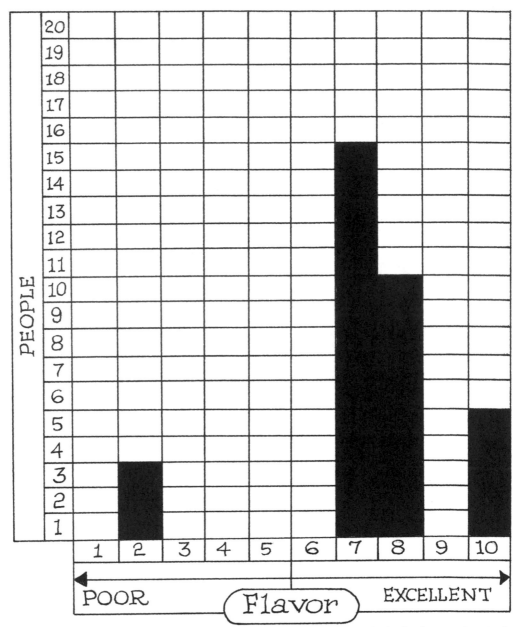

THE NUMBERS ON THE LEFT SIDE REPRESENT THE NUMBER OF PEOPLE WHO SAID THE SAME THING ABOUT THE SODA. (IN THIS SURVEY 5 PEOPLE SAID THE FLAVOR WAS EXCELLENT.)

You can make a similar graph to show the results of your own survey. Make a different graph for each characteristic you surveyed.

Step 1. Draw a vertical line down the left-hand side of a sheet of graph paper, and draw a horizontal line near the bottom of the page. The vertical line represents the number of people who have responded. The horizontal line represents the grading scale.

Step 2. Each square on the vertical line represents 1 person.

Step 3. On the horizontal line mark off 10 squares. On this scale, 10 represents an excellent grade for the characteristic you are studying, whereas 1 represents a poor grade.

In the drawing the characteristic is graded from 1 to 10. It also could be graded 1 to 5 or from 1 to 3.

Interpreting Your Results

A graph is useful because you can see all of your results at once. Instead of having to look at a whole stack of individual surveys, or a whole page of numbers, the graph provides an immediate picture of the relative number of responses. Look at the graphs of the flavor and the sweetness surveys on pages 74–75. You could conclude that the recipe's flavor was all right but that it needed less sugar. This is because a majority of the people indicated they liked the flavor, but these same people thought that the sweetness of the drink was a little too high.

By comparing graphs, you can also learn something about the way different groups respond. The graphs on pages 76–77 were put together by fifth-grade students who tested their soda with both second-grade and sixth-grade students. Notice that the responses from the sixth-grade students

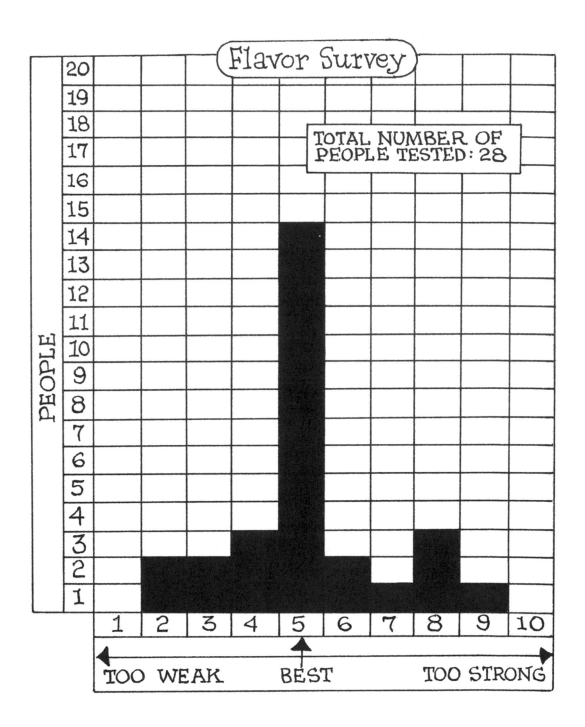

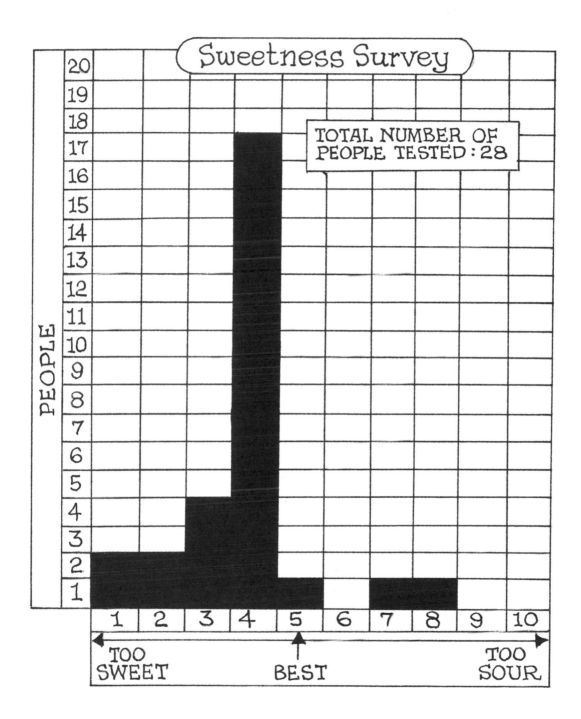

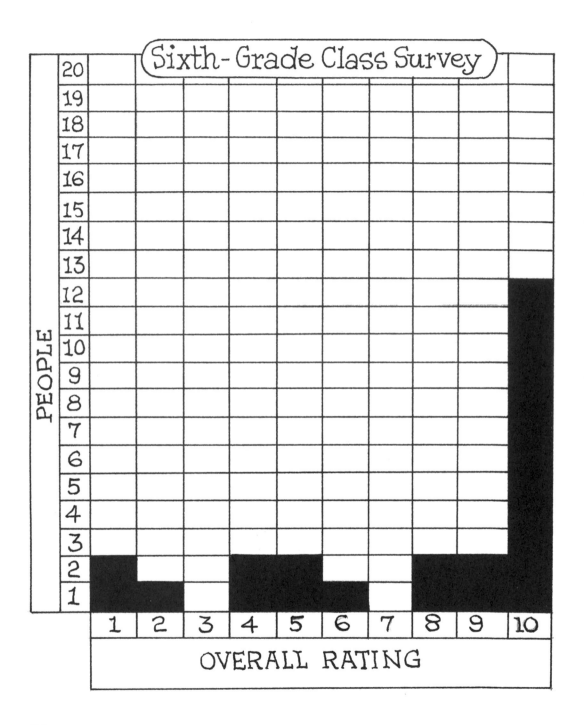

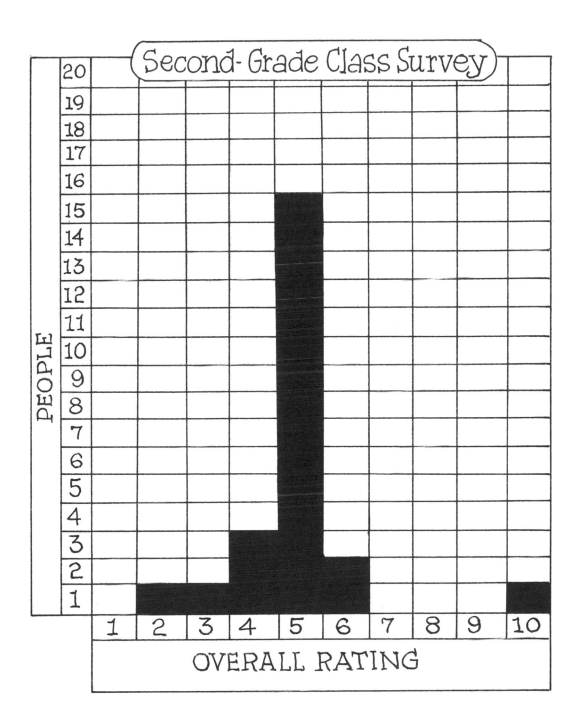

are more spread out, showing a range of opinions about the different characteristics of the soda. There is more agreement in the second-grade class. One way you might interpret this is to say that the younger students are more easily influenced by their friends and also are less concerned about specific characteristics. Older students and adults have more experience with different kinds of drinks and may be better able to identify and judge the separate characteristics of a drink. Therefore, they are more likely to say that they like the drink, but they are also more likely to point out one characteristic of the drink that could be improved. If you were only looking at pages of ungraphed responses from both groups, it would be hard to notice this difference between the grade levels. Placing the two graphs together allows you to see this difference all at once.

FINDING OUT ABOUT COMMERCIAL SODAS

By now you should have a pretty good idea what makes a good soda. The flavor is certainly the most important characteristic, but the relative proportions of each ingredient can make a big difference in whether people like a drink or not. Too much or too little of the flavor or sweetness and they will reject it.

Now that you have designed your own recipe, you can compare it with commercial sodas. Did you come up with proportions similar to those in the sodas you find in the supermarket?

To find out, you can do some tests to see if you can determine approximately how much color, sugar, flavor, and fizz are in commercial sodas. In this section, you will find out how to do this. Before reading on, though, try to come up with a few techniques of your own.

MEASURING COLOR IN COMMERCIAL SODAS

Brown sodas, such as cola and root beer, are colored in a special way, and they are not easy to match. But many other sodas—red, orange, yellow, and purple—are colored with food coloring, and these colors are simpler to match. Can you determine how much food color you would have to add to a 1-liter bottle of seltzer water to match the color of a commercial soda? Since 1 liter is a lot of liquid, you will be using smaller amounts of water in this set of experiments. Then you can multiply the results.

You will need:
    10 clear plastic cups, 9-ounce size
    1 box of food color (This is usually available in the spice section of most
        supermarkets.)
    metric measuring cup
    spoon
    commercial sodas having red, orange, and yellow colors
    water

Getting Started

Why not try your own ideas first and see what kind of results you obtain? Then you can try the following procedure.

Step 1. Pour 100 milliliters of a commercial soda into 1 clear plastic cup.

Step 2. Pour 100 milliliters of water into 5 clear plastic cups.

Step 3. Add drops of food color to each cup of water in increasing amounts. If you are trying to match a pure color, such as red or yellow, add 1 drop at a time. If you are trying to match a blended color, such as purple or orange, add 1 drop of each of the 2 required colors at a time.

Experiments to Try

Examine the color of the water in the 5 cups, and compare the colors with the color of the commercial soda. Make sure to use the same perspective when you make your comparisons.

• How closely do the colors match? Would you have to use half drops to better approximate the color of the commercial soda?

• Does it make a difference whether you look at the test cups and the cup of commercial soda from the side or the top? Does the intensity of the color look the same no matter which way you look at the cup?

• Is it easier or harder to match the color of cloudy sodas?

What's Happening?

The red sodas, such as strawberry and raspberry, do not have much food color added to them; some brands appear to have about 1 drop per 100 milliliters of water. Ten times this number (10 drops) would give the amount needed to color 1 liter of soda because 1,000 milliliters equals 1 liter. Grape soda has about 1 or 2 drops of red and 1 or 2 drops of blue for each 100 milliliters of water.

The way you view the containers in the experiments is important. If you were to compare your test solutions in the cups with the soda in a bottle, you might err a little. Therefore, the two solutions should be in the same kind of container when making comparisons. And you need to compare the same quantity of liquid, from the same viewpoint, so that you are seeing the color in the same volume of solution. To help you to understand why, try looking at a full, tall glass of colored water from the top and then from the side. When you look at the solution from the top, you will see a solution that appears darker than when you look at it from the side. Looking at it from the top, you are seeing all the colored substance in the solution. Looking at it from the side, you are only seeing a cross section of the solution and a smaller quantity of the colored substance.

This is why you should make your comparison using the same kinds of containers and looking at them from the same viewpoint.

Some soda colors will be hard to match with food colors. For instance, you may not be able to match the color of a yellow soda even though you are using yellow food color. This is because the soda manufacturer may use different color sources. Sometimes the label indicates the color used with a pigment number. These pigments may not be exactly the same as those in the bottle of food color you buy in the supermarket.

Sodas with fruit juices added to them tend to be cloudy. These are hard to match with pure food color, because solutions with pure food color in them are clear. Try adding some orange juice or lemon juice to your test solutions to see if you can match the cloudiness of the commercial soda.

MEASURING GAS IN COMMERCIAL SODAS

As soon as you twist the cap off a soda bottle, gas comes rushing out and bubbles keep forming in the liquid. To measure the amount of gas, you need a way to untwist the cap and capture the escaping gas.

This section describes two methods of measuring gas, but before you read them, see if you can think of a measuring technique yourself.

THE INFLATED-BALLOON METHOD

You will need:
- several unopened 1-liter bottles of soda
- 1 package of large round balloons with large necks
  (Look for balloons that can be filled with helium.)
- 1 large bucket
- large roasting pan or plastic dishpan
- measuring cup
- rubber bands
- water

Getting Started

Step 1.   Stretch the balloon, especially the neck, several times to make the
           rubber more elastic.

Step 2.   Ask someone to hold an unopened soda bottle while you stretch the
           neck of the balloon over the neck of the bottle. Break a rubber band,
           wrap it around the neck of the balloon as shown in the drawing, and
           then tie it.

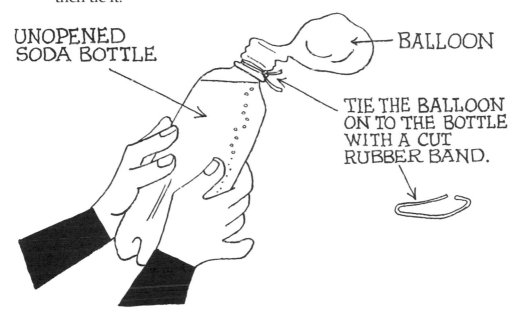

UNOPENED
SODA BOTTLE.

BALLOON

TIE THE BALLOON
ON TO THE BOTTLE
WITH A CUT
RUBBER BAND.

Step 3.   Being careful not to cut the rubber or pull the neck of the balloon
           over the cap, reach through the elastic of the balloon and loosen the
           bottle cap slightly. *Do not remove the cap.* Just untwist it until gas
           rushes into the balloon, inflating it. Hold the neck of the balloon very
           tightly, and shake the bottle. Keep doing this until there is no more
           foaming at the top of the liquid. Carefully remove the gas-filled
           balloon from the bottle and tie the neck so that no gas escapes.

Step 4.   Set the large roasting pan or dishpan on the floor. Put the bucket in the pan, and fill the bucket *to the brim* with water.

Step 5.   Submerge the gas-filled balloon in the bucket of water so that all of it is under the water.

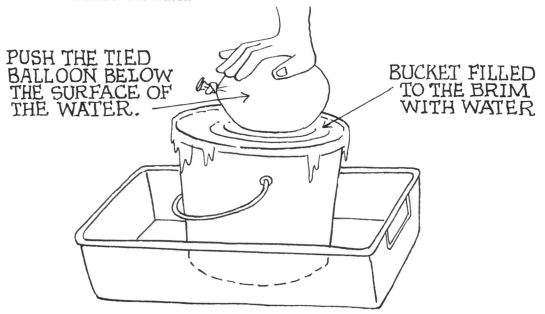

PUSH THE TIED BALLOON BELOW THE SURFACE OF THE WATER.

BUCKET FILLED TO THE BRIM WITH WATER

This will cause the water in the bucket to overflow into the pan. Measure the amount of water in the pan by pouring it into a measuring cup. The volume of gas that escaped from the soda and entered the balloon is about equal to the amount of water in the cup.

THE DISPLACEMENT METHOD

You will need:
   1 piece of plastic tubing, 3 feet long by $\frac{1}{4}$ inch in diameter (This is available at most hardware stores.)
   1 large bucket

1 empty 2- or 3-liter soda bottle

several unopened 1-liter bottles of soda

1 large round balloon with a large neck (Look for balloons that can be
   filled with helium.)

rubber band

water

Getting Started

Step 1.   Fill a bucket about half full with water.

Step 2.   Fill the empty soda bottle with water. Place your hand over the
          opening so that water can't run out. Then tip the bottle over and place
          it in the bucket of water. Remove your hand.

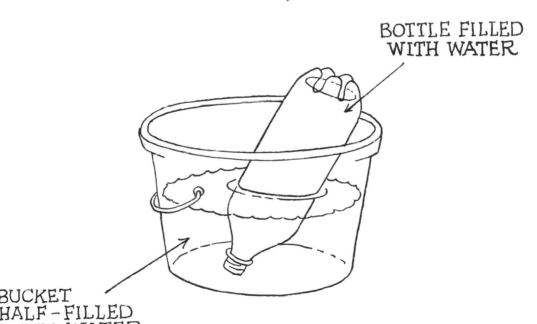

BOTTLE FILLED
WITH WATER

BUCKET
HALF-FILLED
WITH WATER

Step 3.   Slide 1 end of the plastic tubing into the bottle in the bucket.

Step 4.   Cut the balloon at the bottom as shown in the drawing.

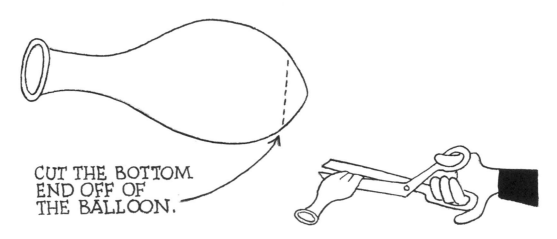

CUT THE BOTTOM
END OFF OF
THE BALLOON.

Secure the cut end of the balloon to the free end of the plastic tubing with the rubber band.

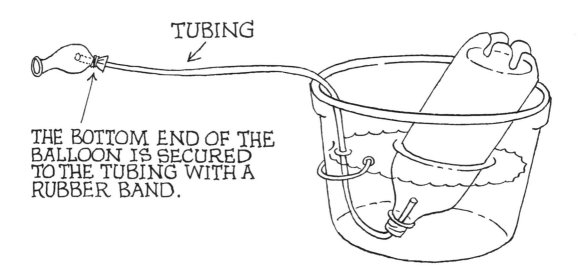

TUBING

THE BOTTOM END OF THE
BALLOON IS SECURED
TO THE TUBING WITH A
RUBBER BAND.

Step 5. Place the neck of the balloon over the neck of the unopened bottle of soda. Being careful not to cut the rubber or pull the neck of the balloon over the cap, reach through the elastic of the balloon and loosen the bottle cap slightly. *Do not remove the cap.* Just untwist it until gas rushes into the balloon, inflating it. As the gas comes out, it will push water out of the bottle that is in the bucket. Hold the neck of the balloon very tightly, and shake the bottle of soda. Keep doing this until there is no more bubbling from the bottle in the bucket.

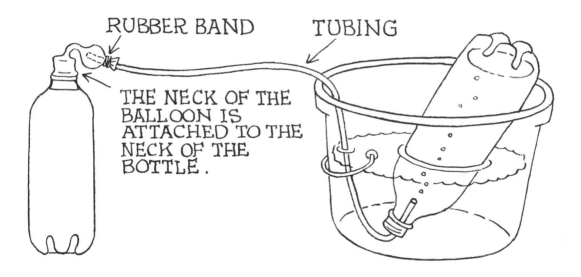

RUBBER BAND   TUBING

THE NECK OF THE BALLOON IS ATTACHED TO THE NECK OF THE BOTTLE.

Step 6. Place your hand over the opening of the bottle in the bucket so that water can't run out. Then turn the bottle right side up and set it on a table. Measure how much water it takes to fill the bottle up again. The volume of gas that escaped from the soda is about the same as the volume of water needed to refill the bottle.

Experiments to Try

Each time you do a new experiment, you should use a new balloon. That's because after balloons have been stretched once or twice they change their *elasticity,* or stretchiness.

- Does the volume of gas depend on whether the soda is very cold or at room temperature?
- Try the experiment again using an unopened 2-liter bottle of soda. How much more gas is collected from the 2-liter bottle than from the 1-liter bottle of soda?

What's Happening?

With either the inflated-balloon method or the displacement method, the moment you untwist the bottle cap, gas comes rushing out of the bottle and many bubbles form. Shaking the bottle releases more gas, and the bubbles keep forming for several minutes. Room-temperature soda produces more gas than cold soda. At the factory the gas is added to cold soda. This allows the manufacturer to dissolve more gas in the soda. As the solution's temperature rises, the gas has a greater tendency to leave the solution.

While both methods will give you a good idea of the amount of gas the soda contains, each technique has its limitation. Collecting the gas in the balloon doesn't give a true measure of the volume because the elastic balloon squeezes the gas and therefore compresses the volume of gas. A non-elastic container doesn't squeeze and compress the gas. The 2-liter bottle displacement method allows the gas to be under ordinary pressure; however, a small amount of gas probably dissolves in the water as it bubbles through. This gas remains in the bucket and is never measured. For these experiments, however, the displacement method is more accurate.

If you were to take the bottle with the balloon attached to its neck and turn it upside down, you could swish the solution around and mix it with the gas in the balloon. You might be able to get some of the gas to redissolve in the solution. However, since this gas was originally under a lot of pressure and now it isn't, it will not all go back into the solution. The balloon would have to be squeezed very hard to force the gas into the solution.

The amount of gas collected from a 2-liter bottle will be much more than from a 1-liter bottle, but it won't necessarily be twice the amount. Because some of the gas dissolves in the water as it escapes and because the method of collecting the gas is somewhat inaccurate, it is difficult to make a true comparison.

MEASURING FLAVOR AND SWEETNESS IN COMMERCIAL SODAS

Finding the relative amount of color in a commercial soda is not difficult since your eye is very good at noticing small differences in concentration. It is a greater challenge to determine the relative amount of flavor and sweetness in sodas because it is hard to taste those two characteristics separately. In this activity, the flavor and sweetness are added separately, but they are tested and compared together.

You will need:
 1 package of clear plastic cups, 9-ounce size
 set of measuring spoons
 metric measuring cup
 spoon
 sugar
 grape juice
 1 bottle of grape soda
 water

Getting Started

Step 1. Measure out 100 milliliters of water into each of 10 clear plastic cups.

Step 2. Add 1 teaspoon of grape juice to the first cup, 2 teaspoons to the second cup, 3 teaspoons to the third cup, 4 teaspoons to the fourth cup, and so on, to the tenth cup.

Step 3. Add 1 teaspoon of sugar to each cup and stir well.

Experiments to Try

• Compare the taste of the solution in each cup with that of the commercial soda. Is there 1 cup that is similar in flavor and sweetness to the commercial soda?

• Start over again with clean cups and repeat Steps 1 and 2 above. For Step 3, add 2 teaspoons of sugar to each cup, stir well, and taste. Is there 1 cup that tastes like the commercial soda?

What's Happening?

There are a number of ways that you could have tried to find out how much flavor and sugar are in the commercial soda. You could have started with water and added the flavor and the sugar 1 teaspoon at a time, until you had a solution that was similar to the commercial soda. But when you add 2 ingredients at once, you may reach a point where you have enough flavor but not enough sugar, or the other way around.

Another method would be to try to match the sweetness of the commercial soda by adding teaspoons of sugar to water until the two taste similar, and then adding enough grape juice to match the flavor of the commercial soda. But grape juice and many other juices have natural sugar in them, so your test solution would be too sweet.

The advantage of the technique you used here is that you can systematically change the amount of each ingredient in known amounts. It takes longer than the other methods, but it gives you more control over the experiment and more accurate results.

When food scientists test unknown solutions in a laboratory, they use special instruments or chemical tests that are designed specifically for each ingredient. That way they can find out exactly how much of each ingredient is present in the unknown solution.

BECOMING A FOOD SCIENTIST

The four sections in this book approach sodas in three different ways. The first part showed you how certain ingredients can be extracted from natural substances. The second part showed you how you can add fizz. The third part helped you combine these ingredients to make your own soda, which may be similar to or even better than the commercial ones. The fourth part showed how the ingredients in commercial sodas can be measured.

You now have some idea how commercial sodas are put together. The processes you followed in this book are not identical to those used by manufacturers, but they give you some sense of what is involved. Along the way, you gained experience that will help you understand some basic concepts in chemistry and mathematics.

Cooking can be an opportunity to learn about other kinds of scientific thinking and knowledge. For instance, ice-cream making with simple containers can help you understand something about heat transfer. Baking cakes and making bread can help you understand something about chemical reactions. Look in your local library for *Baking Chemistry,* by Bernie Zubrowski, and for other books on how to do fun science in your kitchen. But remember—whenever you do some experimenting in the kitchen, have an adult around to help you and make sure you are following safe cooking and experimenting procedures.